LET'S IMAGINE ...

Spontaneity Training Exercises
for Creative Facilitators

devised by

Ron Wiener

www.lulu.com

First published 2012

by Lulu.com

ISBN 978-1-4717-1305-7

Available from www.lulu.com

Acknowledgements

My thanks to the group at '7' – a weekly social improvisation group for the over-50s that I have facilitated for a number of years. Nearly all of these exercises were first tried out with them.

My thanks also to Di Adderley for her excellent editing job and getting the text print ready and also to Simon Mulligan for the cartoons.

Contents

Introduction

The Exercises:

INTRODUCTION

Spontaneity is the spark that starts the process. Creativity is the effort that produces the finished work of art.

A musician hears a couple of notes in his head as he walks along – the hard creative work is turning this into a fully composed piece of music. A painter comes across a scene and gets a flash of inspiration and then spends days translating this into a painting.

This book contains many spontaneity exercises to use in groups – they are the spark to get things going. The creativity comes from you and the group in developing the exercises so they lead into the work of the group. None of the exercises requires any props.

Unlike other books in this genre which tend to be prescriptive, laying down a list of instructions – when and how to be used by how many – this book works on the assumption that exercises work best when the trainer adapts them and puts something of themselves and of the group's experience into their execution.

Three techniques that are useful in exploring these exercises are:

1. **Role Reversal** – where participants swap roles so that they can see the world from another's perspective;

2. **Doubling** or **Shadowing** – where another group member stands or sits by one of the participants and gives voice to the unspoken thoughts and feelings that the participant might have;

3. **Tagging** – a term borrowed from wrestling, where a group member is warmed up by the action, identifies with a participant's role and comes and takes it over.

As mentioned in the acknowledgements, the social improvisation group for the over-50's that I have facilitated for a number of years at '7', an arts and community centre in Leeds, became skilled at developing scenes, adding roles and exploring the different dimensions of their characters.

****

Ron Wiener is a senior sociodrama trainer, group facilitator, organisational consultant and community theatre director and producer. He is the author of *Drugs and Schoolchildren* (1970, Longmans), *Community Action: The Belfast Experience* (1978, Farset Co-operative Press), *Creative Training* (1997, Jessica Kingsley) and co-editor of *Sociodrama in a Changing World* (2011, Lulu.com) plus numerous book chapters, articles and training videos.

THE EXERCISES

Advertising

Group in pairs.

Each pair has to devise an advertisement for either a real or an imaginary product. For example:

- *different coloured tyres to match the paint trim on cars*

- *reading glasses with a buzzer system to make them easier to find.*

Each pair in turn then shows their ad, as if it's a TV commercial, to the whole group,

The majority of the rest of the group then become a focus group discussing both the product and the ad.

A small number of the rest of the group become the representatives of the manufacturing company who comment on the focus group's discussion.

If the group is small in number then the pair who showed their ad can become the manufacturer's representatives.

Art gallery

- Some of the group become sculptures of varying complexity. The rest of the group become visitors to the gallery commenting on the sculptures. An added twist is to introduce the sculptor who then has to explain the meaning of each piece.

- The whole of the room becomes a gallery showing contemporary art and the group, in sub-groups, become the visitors commenting on everything in the room – the coffee mugs, a piece of blutac on the wall – as if they are exhibits. An added twist here is for the gallery to have a guide who has to explain the significance of the exhibition.

Auditions

A television channel is looking for two presenters for a new reality TV show – the group can make up the title.

A small number of people become the interviewers, the rest become pairs bidding to become the presenters.

The presenters need time to prepare their auditions. Pairs can be given additional prompt scenarios, such as:

- *You have personal issues with each other which emerge during the audition;*

- *There are gender/racial or other differences that emerge;*

- *You think this audition is beneath you and you are only here because of economic hard times;*

- *You are completely wrong for the show, i.e. if the show is aimed at young people the presenters become old age pensioners.*

During the audition process, the interviewers have the option of how they will play their roles:

- *Disinterested*

- *Challenging*

- *Enthusiastic*

Celebrations

The group is divided into pairs or threes who are out celebrating an event such as St. Valentine's Day or a birthday.

Each sub-group makes up a story that they then enact.

One option is that the pair to the right then pick up the story one week later and the pair to the right of them a further month away and so on.

Or you could also have the pair to the left telling the story one week before.

Cons

Work in small groups.

Here the aim is for one, two or three people to become con artists of some description. They must convince one or two other people to part with their money.

The 'suckers' could be:

- *Senior citizens*
- *Tourists in a foreign country*
- *Single person householders*

The setting could be:

- *A telephone call*
- *An ATM / hole in the wall machine*
- *A railway station*

Cook-off

Group is sub-divided into groups of around five to ten people.

Each group has one or two cooks.

The other members of the group become the ingredients for a meal devised by the cooks.

The aim is to be the team whose cooks first get their meal ready for cooking in an oven or stove.

The ingredients, such as vegetables are free to enact their roles however they wish. They could hinder or help the cook(s) and may bicker amongst themselves.

Deathbed confessions

In pairs, *A* and *B*.

A confesses to *B* either a real or imaginary

- *Regret, or*
- *An unfulfilled desire*

and *B* does the same to *A*. The pair then choose one of the two scenes to show to the rest of the group, who then enact the story.

Facilitators need to be aware that if a 'real' issue is chosen then it is possible that the enactment will become psychodramatic and may well move beyond being a simple warm-up exercise.

Dialogues

A variety of options for starter scripts in pairs:

- *A has to tell B not to use a mobile phone in the quiet carriage on a train*
- *Middle-aged white man tries to tell a teenager from a different ethnic background to turn their music down on a bus*
- *A and B compare clothes while aiming to top the other one in terms of style and fashion*
- *Male teenager tries to persuade a girl that it's cool to have sex;*
- *Couple argues about who forgot to put out the rubbish last night when really the quarrel is about the state of their relationship*
- *A bumps into B - an old acquaintance whose name they can't remember*
- *Couple argues over whether this is the right time to;*
    - *start trying to have a baby*
    - *put a parent into a nursing home*
    - *go on holiday given the state of the economy*
    - *build an extension to their house*
    - *put money into a pension plan.*

Doctor's waiting room

A number of people are sitting in a doctor's waiting room, all studiously ignoring each other. There is a receptionist at one end of the setting.

A new person comes in asking for an appointment. The receptionist wants to know what the problem is. The new person is reluctant to say.

Their interchange opens the way for the rest of the waiting room to start talking to each other about their ailments / waiting room procedures etc.

Drama scripts

In pairs or trios, sub-groups are given the first two lines of a drama which they then have to develop. Some examples are given below:

A: *I don't know how we have got to this situation but it can't continue.*

B: *Well it's gone on for so long I don't see any reason why it shouldn't go on forever.*

A: *You have more to do with them then I do. It isn't fair!*

B: *Well life isn't always fair it's just how it has turned out.*

A: *I think you should have said what you really feel. It's all very well to turn the other cheek but sometimes you need to stand up and be counted.*

B: *You think I should have slapped him?*

A: *It's your turn to do it.*

B: *No it isn't.*

C: *I agree with A – it's your turn B – we're always being landed with it.*

A: *Getting older isn't great*

B: *You can't call yourself old at your age.*

A possible next step is to put people into new groups of three and get them to devise a new story with three characters, again using one of the starter scripts.

A final step is to divide the group into fours, each group with one of the stories which now has to have four characters.

Ex-lover

Exercise in threes.

A couple walks in a park: they meet an ex-lover of one of them.

Each trio prepares their version of the scene. The trios then take turns to show their scene to the whole group.

Possible extensions:

- The facilitator chooses one of the versions, which has energy, for the whole group to work with and allows it to develop into further scenes in which other roles may emerge;

- The group decides which of the scenes they would like to work with more, and each trio then shows what the next scene in the story might be.

Exploring a relationship

The group is divided into two rows of people facing each other with each person paired off with another in the opposite row.

The first pair start a story about a relationship. For example,

- *divorcing couple*
- *first date*
- *couple uncertain whether to take the relationship further.*

First pair are free to determine the content.

After a short period, the facilitator gets the next pair to take the story on. They have to pick it up from the exact point where the first pair finished.

And so on through all the pairs.

With the last pair the story can then be expanded via tagging and / or doubling and the introduction of new characters, such as:

- *parent;*
- *previous lovers.*

Fairy stories

Sub-groups make up or adapt a fairy story so that it is appropriate to the present time. For example:

There was a girl who had two stepsisters. Her mother had died and her father had married again. He was often away as he worked for a multi-national company. Whenever he left, the stepmother would turn against the girl and favour her own children. For example, she bought each of her daughters a new iPad, while the girl was only given crayons and some scrap paper.

The two stepsisters were invited to go to a party given by a famous local DJ while the girl was going to be left at home on her own. However her favourite aunt was also going to the party and she hatched a plan. Auntie said to the girl that she would take her iPad with her. If the girl could borrow one of her stepsister's iPads then she could Skype with the aunt and see everything that was happening.

At the party, the DJ noticed the aunt Skype-ing and said "Who is that beautiful girl with the glass shoes that you're talking to?" and the aunt replied that it was her niece. The next day the DJ knocked at the door and said he had come to call on the girl with the glass shoes. The stepsisters said there was no one like that here but the girl crept in and when the DJ saw her it was love at first sight.

As each sub-group narrates their story, the rest of the group enacts it.

Hairdresser

This setting provides a variety of possible scenes for pairs to explore:

- A *persuades* B *to have a haircut they don't want*
- *Hairdresser* A *who won't shut up while cutting* B*'s hair*
- *Hairdresser who forgot to tell customer that they have put up prices before they started cutting*
- *Customer complaining to hairdresser about quality of cut*
- B *back from hairdresser has to defend terrible haircut to partner*
- A *and* B *are partners in a hairdressing business – A wants to change business from single sex to multi-sex (or some other alteration), B resists.*

Scenes can be extended by having:

- *Other customers who join in the discussion*
- *Partners of the customer present*
- *The customer is a child / teenager with a parent present.*

Hotel rooms

In groups of three:

Exercise 1

A couple (who may or may not be married) go away to a hotel together for the weekend. One of them invites a friend along who doesn't get on with their partner. When the couple get to their hotel they find that, rather then having one single and one double room they have been given a triple bedroom and the hotel is full. Create a story around this issue.

Exercise 2

A couple with a child are at a hotel where the child has to share a room with the parents. Two possible scenarios:

- Couple are pretending all is well in their relationship but really they are about to separate and are trying to keep this from the child

- The child is a teenager who is most reluctant to share a room with the parents.

Obviously the group can create its own story as well.

Exercise 3

A couple are in a hotel room. They have ordered room service but it is a long time coming. Eventually the food/drink is brought but the waiter / waitress arrives is reluctant to leave without a tip, which the couple are unwilling to give.

How not to …

Groups of two showing how not to:

- *Do a supervision session*
- *Chat up someone at a singles bar*
- *Tell someone their breath smells or they have bad body odour*
- *Tell a person they are about to lose their job*
- *Inform a partner that they have given you an STD (sexually transmitted disease)*
- *Inform a person that their bank account was credited with £2k by mistake when that money has already been spent.*

The choice will be determined by the content of the session that follows.

Interpreters

Groups of three:

- A *speaks no English (or whatever the national language is)*
- B *is the interpreter*
- C *is the person that* A *wishes to communicate with.*

Possible settings

- *Doctor's surgery*
- *Dating situation*
- *Children's exchange visit*

Group switch around so everyone takes a turn at each of the three roles.

Joining in

Two people in the group come centre stage and start a scene. When they mention a third character, a member of the watching group moves into the action and becomes this new character. The three then continue the scene but create a space for a fourth role: again, this new role is spontaneously taken up by another group member. This continues until all the group members have a role in the story.

Entry into the scene of each new character must make sense in terms of the developing story line.

When all have joined, one of the-sub plots becomes the lead-off for a new story.

In this way, a story which started off in a breast implant clinic ended up having Prince Charles, Camilla and Prince William discussing the succession to the throne on the Queen's death. They were joined by Prince Harry, Kate Middleton, Princess Anne, a TV interviewer and her co-host.

Laundry

In pairs, *A* and *B*.

Each pair decides on their relationship.

A has washed *B*'s clothes in the washing machine but has included a garment that has run which means that *B*'s clothes have gone 'pink' – or the pairs can come up with an equally appalling tragedy.

A and *B* now have a conversation / argument about what has happened.

If one of these conversations happens in a public space then there is the option of the rest of the group taking on other roles in the launderette (customers / workers / overflowing machines etc.)

Modeling

Group is divided into groups of three.

In each trio the roles are:

- *a photographer*
- *a model*
- *an announcer / voice-over.*

Stage One:

Each group devises a short scene in which the photographer poses the model that is showing off the clothes he / she is actually wearing while the announcer provides a commentary. They show the scene to the other groups

Stage Two:

Stage One is repeated with roles rotating until all three people have played each of the roles

Stage Three:

Each group chooses one model. The models then promenade down an improvised cat walk while the rest of the group become the commenting audience.

Murder

A murder scene is created by the group, such as:

The Lord of the manor is found dead in the morning under suspicious circumstances.

Everyone else is a suspect. The group creates pairs of characters, which could include:

- *Lady Dowager – a right wing politician / visiting politician*
- *Son 1 with daughter-in-law*
- *Son 2 – with daughter-in-law*
- *Daughter with son-in-law*
- *Maid & Gardener.*

Each pair has to find a motivation as to why they might have committed the murder and an alibi to prove they couldn't have.

There are also a detective and their assistant who have to find the real murderer. They are allowed to eavesdrop on each of the suspect pairs.

Then the detectives have to interview the suspects either individually, in pairs or in a group.

Each suspect has to adapt their story to make sense of their alibi in the light of what previous suspects have said. They also need to try and convince the detectives that someone else had a better motive and opportunity to commit the crime.

The detectives have to deduce who the murderers were.

New technology

Scenario 1

Person A, who is technologically naïve, tries to explain a problem with their TV or Broadband to a call-centre operator.

Scenario 2

Shop assistant in a computer store attempts to persuade an individual, couple or family of the merits of a new computer / mobile phone / tablet etc. An additional option here, if one uses the family scene, is for the family to include a young person who is computer literate and who embarrasses the parents by knowing more then they do about new technology.

Scenario 3

A family scene: the parents are trying to limit their children's use of social media – Facebook, Twitter etc.

Objects

Pairs or small groups.

In a house fire, what object in your house would you save?

Become that object and describe to the others in the sub-group:

- *Why you would be saved*

- *Your meaning for the 'owner'*

- *How you feel about other objects that were not saved.*

The other(s) in the group can ask follow up questions.

New pairs or sub-groups.

Become one of the objects that would be left behind and describe:

- *How you feel about not being chosen*

- *Why you were chosen to live in this house in the first place.*

Open door

For pairs to start with, then possible involvement of most of the group.

Two chairs are placed indicating a door opening.

One side could be:

- *An office*
- *The hallway of a domestic dwelling.*

A comes to the door; *B* is on the inside. They improvise a scene. For example:

A schoolchild is sent to the head teacher's office. Child says 'he made me do it.'

Other characters can then enter the story, so in the above scene, there could be:

- *The schoolchild's mother*
- *The other child from 'he made me do it'*
- *The other child's mother*
- *A form teacher.*

Overheard sentences

The facilitator collects half-heard bits of conversations while out and about. The group is divided into pairs or trios. Each sub-group improvises a story using the collected sentences: they become the couple having the original conversation. For example:

- *He swears more than he eats.*
- *She didn't, did she?*
- *I couldn't believe that it had happened again.*
- *I'm not going back there.*
- *The hotel was not what we expected. I wouldn't go there if I were you.*

Another pair then becomes the people who overheard the first pair. This second pair creates a scene where they comment on the first pair's conversation. For example, if the first pair had been sitting in a restaurant, the second pair might have been a couple at another table, overhearing the first conversation: back at home they reflect on their day.

Alternatively, the pairs can each make up a sentence and give it to the next pair to enact. In one exercise, the sentences that sub-groups came up with were:

- *I was expecting a romantic present.*
- *I want to pull your trousers down.*
- *How many times do I have to tell you?*

Overtly polite

Pairs or trios.

A / B are *C*'s neighbours.

C asks *A / B* *"How are you?"*

A / B wants to tell *C* that something serious has happened in their life, for example a close relative has died, but they are constrained by the rituals of 'polite' conversation.

C senses something is wrong but is equally constrained.

So the conversation might, for example, have to talk about the unspoken through the metaphor of the weather.

Photos

Subdivide the group.

Each sub-group poses itself as a group of people in a photo.

This can then take a number of avenues:

- The rest of the group can describe what they see
- The people in the photo can describe who they are and what is happening
- Other roles can be created – the photographer, onlookers, people viewing the photo at a gallery or a family gathering
- Other group members can join the photo, engaging with the original participants
- The photographer could be showing the photo to his or her friends/family etc.

Privacy

Group divided into fours, each four to consist of two pairs.

The two couples have agreed to go on holiday together to a cottage.

One couple is open-minded about open access to the bathroom, the other couple is more prudish and believes in locked doors.

The couples spend sometime working out which roles they want and what their background to the trip away is.

Scene One – at the bathroom door, where the conflict between access to the bathroom becomes clear.

Scene Two – each couple separately discuss their reflection on scene one.

Scene Three – couples meet to discuss how they will negotiate their differences over the rest of the holiday.

Possible further scene – the prudish couples from the different fours turn out to be neighbours, who meet to discuss what happened on their respective holidays. The same with the more open-minded couples.

In one playing of this story, a couple who were nudists went away with a more prudish couple and the compromise reached in scene three was that half the week they would spend naked and half the week clothed.

Quiz show

The group is divided into pairs or small groups. Each pair chooses its own area of expertise and devises three questions that others in the rest of the group might have a chance of answering.

Each pair then asks its three questions in turn and each of the other pairs compete to see how many questions they can answer.

The facilitator keeps score and acts as the quizmaster.

The winners are the pair who give the most right answers.

Reminiscences

One group member volunteers to be an imaginary older person reflecting on their life.

As they tell a scene from their past life, the rest of the group enact it and then embellish it.

Then a new person takes centre stage. They can either describe another scene from the life the first person started with or they can create an entirely new character.

The scenes will be more psychodramatic if the protagonist is asked, or volunteers, to describe a scene from their own life. In this case it is possible for the protagonist to show a number of scenes so they end up seeing a time line of crucial events in their history.

Shoes

Ask each member of the group to talk about the shoes they are wearing:

- *Where were they purchased?*

- *Why are they being worn today?*

- *How much did they cost?*

Then divide the group into pairs by asking people to become their shoes and choose another pair of shoes they would be interested in meeting.

In pairs, remaining in role as the shoes, take it in turns to describe:

- *The different pairs of shoes your 'owner' has and where you fit in.*

- *Are there some shoes that are never chosen?*

- *Are there 'racial' overtones, in that the owner prefers one colour to another?*

- *Are some shoes in your owner's wardrobe stuck away all winter and never see daylight?*

Singing

The group comes up with a number of songs that most people know.

The group then sings each song in turn.

After each song, sub-groups become the singer explaining the (made-up) incidents that led to the song being composed and the meaning behind some of the key words.

For example, *You are my Sunshine* could have been originally composed as a beer drinking advertisement.

An additional method is to work with nursery rhymes and deconstruct them as a modern fable.

For example, *Goosey Goosey Gander* is a story about old age abuse.

Soap operas

Ask people to nominate their favourite TV soap opera. Participants are divided into groups on the basis of their favourite soap. Also have a group for people who either don't have a favourite and / or who don't watch soaps.

Then suggest a couple of scenes:

- *Á la Romeo and Juliet: the evening reception after a wedding between a couple from warring families;*

- *A woman discovers she is pregnant after a brief fling with someone who is not a boyfriend / husband.*

Alternatively the sub-groups can work around a 'real' event that is currently happening on TV in their soap.

The sub-groups each have to create a scene to show to the rest of the group.

A further development could be that the 'audience' group becomes a family sitting at home watching the 'TV' scene and then commenting on it (they will need time to create family roles).

Story

The facilitator makes up a story that the group then enacts. After introducing each segment, the facilitator pauses to allow for the group enactment of the story so far. This means that the group might well take the story in a variety of new directions which the facilitator has to follow. For example:

Phil met Bernice at a folk dance evening. He was on his own and espied a group of girls across the room. (Pause for action)

He recognised one of them, Janet, who looked up and saw him. She pointed him out to her friends but he couldn't hear what they said. (Pause)

She came over and asked him if he wanted to join them. (Pause)

He came over and she introduced him to her three friends but he only had eyes for Bernice. (Pause)

The women asked him about himself. (Pause)

Then it was time for the next dance. They all got up and a caller instructed them how to do the next dance. The rest of the audience clapped along. (Pause)

At the end of the evening, Phil was too shy to ask Bernice out and he left on his own. (Pause)

The girls ragged Bernice about how Phil was smitten with her. (Pause)

The next day Phil phoned Janet to get Bernice's number. (Pause)

He phoned her but a man answered and Phil wasn't sure how to respond as the man said Bernice was out. (Pause)

Phil then phoned his mate Roger to ask him what to do. (Pause)

Phil ended up asking Bernice out. (Pause)

She accepted. (Pause)

The next night they met in a crowded local Starbucks. They had to ask another couple if they could sit at their table. The other couple reluctantly agreed. (Pause)

Phil wanted to ask Bernice about the man who had answered the phone and eventually plucked up enough courage to do so. (Pause)

A week later it was double date time with Phil & Roger dating Janet and Bernice. It went well until Phil revealed he had once trained to be a rabbi while Bernice confessed that she still took Catholic communion. (Pause)

A person at the next table then recognised Phil who was embarrassed to see him / her and tried to avoid introducing him / her to the rest of his table. (Pause)

Bernice and Janet then went off to the toilet together where they had a good chat leaving Roger and Phil to do the same.....

I have never reached the end of this story as the group has always improvised an alternative scenario half way through, so I have had to adapt the story and often create new roles in the moment to keep the group engaged.

Swapping sub-groups

The group is divided into pairs or trios.

Each sub-group pairs up with another sub-group (A + B).

Each sub-group then creates a scene, with a role for each person in the sub-group, which they then show to the group as a whole.

Then each pair of sub-groups (A + B) decide together which of their two stories they will work on first.

If it is A's story, then sub-group B has to quickly create what the next scene would be that follows on from A's original scene.

Each of these scenes are then shown to the group as a whole.

Then the situation is reversed with A quickly creating the follow up scene to B's original scenario.

Each of these scenes are shown to the group as a whole.

It's possible to extend the whole sequence with the scenes being passed back again to the first group to develop the next part of the story.

Tattoos

In pairs:

- *A* has the name of a previous lover tattooed on their forearm. *B* is the new lover who begins asking questions about the ex- and who might or might not insist on the tattoo being removed;

- Pairs discuss what tattoo they might each like to have if offered a free tattoo as a birthday gift – what would it say, what design, what part of the body.

TV agony aunt

One person is the host of a Jerry Springer or Oprah Winfrey style TV show.

There are two guests who are in conflict.

There is a third guest 'backstage' who is related to the conflict and who can come in and intervene.

The rest of the audience can ask questions and can intervene via doubling and tagging.

For example:

> *The two guests are a mother and a pregnant teenage daughter who have fallen out with each other. Backstage is mother's sister (they don't get on) with whom the daughter wants to live.*

You could add back stage

- *The boyfriend*
- *The boyfriend's mother who also wants the daughter to live with her.*

The foetus could also be given a voice.

The knock at the door

A couple is at home when there is a knock at the door (a gap between two chairs).

On the other side is:

- A young adult who has come to find his parent from a one-night stand that his mother / father had a long time ago. The information about this child's existence is unknown to the other partner;

- A partner from a previous relationship with one of the couple, who has come to see if there is any chance of them getting back together again;

- An angel from God with a message for one of the couple;

- A long-lost acquaintance of one of the couple who asks if they can stay for a few days. The acquaintance can either be someone who brings fond memories or someone with a murky past;

- A stranger who has to make up a story that will gain them entry into the house;

- A detective who has come to arrest one of the couple for an offence that the other knows nothing about.

The self-help book

In pairs, people are invited to come up with a self-help slogan. For example:

- *Happiness is only a step away*
- *Time flies when love dies*
- *Only a fool works with a tool*
- *The internet – you never need to be lonely again*
- *Talking to oneself is only a form of self-love*
- *All revolutions simply repeat history*
- *There's a rainbow around every corner*
- *Look up, look down, go straight.*

They then need to give a short two-minute presentation on the thinking behind the slogan to the rest of the group who could be:

- *an adult education class*
- *a chat show audience (Oprah Winfrey style);*
- *unemployed people*
- *a feminist group*
- *members of a religious group.*

The group is divided into teams of three or four people who will answer questions posed by the facilitator.

Here the exercise is not whether the teams can provide the right answers but is to do with each team having internal conflicts that prevent them functioning properly.

Therefore, before the questioning begins, each team needs to spend some time devising conflicting roles, such as:

- *the swot that no one likes*
- *the jilted lover*

The second stage of the game is where the internal conflicts spill over into disputes between the teams.

Valued People

In small groups, people agree on one historical figure, alive or dead that they would like to bring to life, and shares information about them.

The group as a whole decides where these people might meet:

- *At a dinner party*
- *In the after life*
- *As characters in a historical film.*

One person from each sub-group takes on the agreed character and the scene is enacted. Others can join in as other appropriate roles or can develop / take on any of the agreed historical roles through doubling / tagging.

The scene can then be moved forward. For example:

- *If the first setting was originally a dinner party, we could now be in a historic house where the grandson is explaining to a group of sightseers that this is the room where the 'famous' dinner party took place*
- *People could become the furniture that was in the room at the time – grandfather clock, chairs etc. – reminiscing about the past.*

Worst examples of ...

Group divides up into pairs who create a scene showing the worst ways of being:

- *Marriage guidance counsellors*
- *Life coaches*
- *Financial consultants*
- *Political advisors*
- *Management consultants*
- *Executives firing staff.*

These scenes are then shown to the group as a whole.

Worst ...

Get the group to each find an example of the worst job they have ever had, or worst holiday they have ever been on. Then one person becomes the storyteller while the rest of the group enacts the scene they are telling. The group may spontaneously embellish the story and create further scenes. For example:

The worst job I ever had was working at a fairground stall where children had to roll down ping pong balls into slots and if they got a particular score they won a prize which was an out-of-date box of chocolates. The owner of the stall insisted that I try to get children to have as many goes as possible. I stood it for half a day.

Roles: storyteller (stall holder), stall owner, child

Possible other roles: parent(s), onlookers, box of chocolates, owner's wife

Possible scenes:

1. Stall holder and child

2. Add parent

3. Stall holder and stall owner

4. Stall owner and wife